The Little Fish Guide to Writing Your Own Website

Web copywriting tips
for startups, entrepreneurs, business owners and marketers

Jackie Barrie

Also by Jackie Barrie
The Little Fish Guide to DIY Marketing (2010)
The Little Fish Guide to Networking (2011)

Published by Comms Plus
ISBN 978-0-9565933-5-1

Reviews

"How to Write Your Own Website had me nodding, groaning (at my own stupidity) and laughing out loud – and I ended up with a long list of actions and ideas to improve the copy on my website.

It contains a host of valuable information, whether you are new to websites, or need to review your existing one. Jackie demystifies much of the jargon around websites and makes the whole process very easy to understand. She gets straight to the point – your website is not about YOU; it's about the person reading it, or your ideal clients.

Her advice really got me rethinking my website from the reader's point of view, and I got much clearer on what I want each page and the website as a whole to achieve. I laughed out loud at the section on What Not to Write on Your About Us Page... So obvious on reflection, but exactly the sort of bland blah blah blah that I was in danger of writing on mine.

This book is packed with insight and information that will prove invaluable to anyone who wants to know more about what to write on their website. In just a few pages of great content, Jackie has given me a list of actions that will improve my website and ensure that it gets the results I want for my business, now and in the future."

Dr Emma Sutton, NakedPresenting.co.uk

"Getting your web content wrong can cost you a fortune in lost clients. This terrific little book will save you from making expensive mistakes.

Building your own website? Read it before you write a single word. Briefing someone to create a website for you? Use it to gauge their expertise before you part with your money. Already got a website? Read it to check whether your site is working as well for you as it could.

This book is packed with up-to-the-minute relevant information and it's a delight to read! It provides total clarity as to what works and what doesn't. When it comes to getting your web design and copy 'just right', this little book by Jackie Barrie is the best guide I've ever read."

Angus Whitton, Journey Plan Ltd

"This is a gem of a book. Everything you need to know is set out in plain language with a dash of cheeky humour thrown in. It's filled with all the tips and tricks you'll need to write web copy that appeals to both people AND search engines. After reading it I took a look at my own website and was able to make some important changes right away. Quick and easy to read, I recommend that you get this into your business library immediately!"

Kerrianne Cartmer-Edwards, TheSuccessMindShift.com

Contents

Dedicated to all my lovely clients.

Glossary

There is a lot of jargon in the world of websites. Here are a few of the main terms mentioned in this book that you need to understand before you read on:

Adwords
Paid advertising that appears in the right sidebar of Google search results.

Alt tags
Alternative text used to describe images on websites. Can be seen in some web browsers when you hover the cursor over the picture.

Analytics
Stats that track visitor behaviour on your website. Use them to make informed decisions about layout and content.

H1 tag
The equivalent of Heading 1 in Word styles. Important for SEO.

Keywords, key phrases
The search terms that you want to be found for.

Meta tags
Part of the code that makes up your website; there to be read by search engines, not human beings.

SEO
Search Engine Optimisation, that is, optimising your site's content and tags to help it get found on search.

Introduction

These days, more and more businesses have a Content Management System (CMS) website, or use a blogging tool such as Wordpress or Joomla to build their own.

Quite right too. Why should you have to pay a web professional every time you want to update something?

However, if you don't know what you're doing, you might be losing custom.

I've written hundreds of websites since I launched Comms Plus in 2001, and have compiled almost everything I've learned into this book. You'll find some top tips for effective web content, covering copy, design, video and Search Engine Optimisation (SEO).

I hope you find it useful. Either way, please email your comments to me at jackie@comms-plus.co.uk.

Jackie Barrie

P.S. My thanks to my clients and contacts who granted permission for their case studies and screenshots to be featured in this book.

An **image consultant** had paid thousands to have her website redesigned, and wrote all the copy herself. Despite getting 200 hits per week through Google Adwords and Pay Per Click campaigns, she had no enquiries for two months. I rewrote some key pages, recommended some design changes, and she received six enquiries in the first week including a great corporate opportunity.

A **mortgage adviser** had written his own web copy. Although people were finding his Home page, they were leaving the site in seconds, without clicking through to his sub-pages. He agreed to let me rewrite the Home page as a test. After only a week, his site visitors started clicking through to the next level.

An **eco-cleaner** asked me to write her website so it would be found on a Google search. She told me: "A new client rang me to say: 'I loved your website, it was the most professional of all the cleaning sites I found. And I must congratulate whoever did your copywriting and search engine optimisation. They did a really great job! Whatever cleaning keywords I searched on Google, your site came up, so I decided it was meant to be!'"

Defining copywriting

You might think you can write your own website because you know most about your business and anyway, you learned how to throw a sentence together at school. But copywriting is not the same as 'normal' writing. Copywriting is writing to influence, writing to persuade, writing to change behaviour. Marketing copywriting is any writing for print or screen where you want your readers to **buy your stuff**. Web copywriting is compelling people to do this through the medium of the Internet.

Marketing is so much more than just printed or online communications that hopefully attract attention, arouse interest, generate desire and prompt action. Marketing is **every** aspect of your business that impacts your customer experience.

So, let's make some assumptions. First, that you sell stuff that's worth buying and that there's an audience out there somewhere that wants it. Further, let's assume that you've got a business strategy that defines where you want to go and a marketing strategy that spells out how you plan to get there. This is a rare thing, would you believe, but it's essential to have this in place before you even think about doing any copywriting.

Bear in mind that people are unlikely to read every page of your website; they'll only read the one/s they are interested in. Don't assume they read each page in turn as they would a brochure. Each web page should stand alone with its own heading, picture, body copy and call to action (there's more about 'calls to action' below).

Top tip:
79% web readers scan the text. Only 16% read every word.
Source: NNGroup.com/articles/how-users-read-on-the-web

Long copy v short copy

Top tip:
On-screen, you have less than 3 seconds to make an
impact

A page of web copy on a standard desktop or laptop computer includes about 300 words 'above the fold' (that's the amount you can see without scrolling down, and is named after folded newspapers in a rack). Meanwhile, SEO experts demand about 400 keyword-rich words if you want your web page to be found on search.

Research in the US claims that long copy works better than short copy, although I've never seen similar data relating to the UK. The US approach includes regular testimonials and calls-to-action. In my view, copy should be as long as it needs to do the job, and no longer. The only way to prove what works for you is to test it.

Top tip:
Scrolling down is OK; scrolling sideways is
discouraged.

How to structure web copy

- **Meaningful sub-headings**
    especially the first 2 words
- **1 idea per paragraph**
    <3-5 sentences per paragraph
- **Short sentences**
    <20-25 words per sentence
- **Bulleted lists**
    <7 items per list

Exercise

Compare these two examples of body copy, one for print, one for web. The latter includes exactly the same information but presented in a completely different way.

BEFORE (print)

Enrolling nearly 2,000 students (about 1,200 full-time on-campus), Northwest College is a two-year, residential college offering transfer programs based upon the traditional arts and sciences, and occupational programs which include strong general education requirements. Northwest's 124-acre campus includes 14 instructional buildings, five residence halls and 80 apartments for 825 students, a student center and a mountain field station 50 miles from campus. The college attracts students from throughout the Rocky Mountain Region, more than two dozen states and several foreign countries. Northwest College is accredited by the North Central Association of Colleges and Schools, www.ncacihe.org or 312.263.0456 Location: Northwest serves a diverse region whose economic underpinnings include both tourism and farming/ranching. The college is located in northwest Wyoming, about 70 miles from the east entrance of Yellowstone National Park and 90 miles south of Billings, Montana. Powell is a city of 5,700, the economy of which is based primarily on farming, ranching, oil, and education. Nearby Cody, a popular tourist attraction, provides daily commercial air service.

AFTER (web)

- **Quick Facts about <u>Northwest College</u>:**
  two-year, residential college
  transfer and occupational programs
- nearly **2,000 students**
  1,200 full-time students on-campus
  from over two dozen states and several foreign
  countries
- **124-acre campus**
  14 instructional buildings
  five residence halls
  80 apartments
  mountain field station 50 miles from campus.
- **accredited** by the <u>North Central Association of Colleges and Schools</u> (312.263.0456)
- located in **Powell, Wyoming**, a city of 5,700

Source: Unknown

Note the use of bold, bullet points and <u>hyperlinks</u> to aid on-screen reading. The 'after' format is typical of the presentation style you need for web copywriting.

Before you start

Have you heard the expression 'begin with the end in mind?'

Before you start, you need to know where you want to end up. With copywriting, that means you need to know your objective before you put pen to paper or finger to keyboard. What are you hoping to achieve with this on-screen communication? Because, do you know what? Copywriting is sometimes **not** the answer! Sometimes, what you want just can't be achieved in writing at all - what you need is a phone call or face-to-face meeting or seminar instead.

So first, define your objectives e.g. Make an appointment, sign up for my tipsheet, download a report, phone this number, buy now.

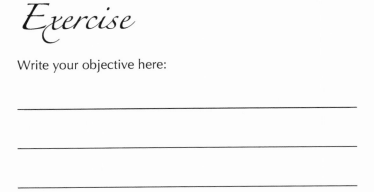

Exercise

Write your objective here:

_____

_____

_____

You may recognise that the above objectives are what's known in the marketing trade as 'calls to action'. If you don't include a call to action in a marketing piece it's not direct response; it's brand awareness. It's not marketing; it's advertising. It doesn't raise sales (at least, not directly); it raises profile. You have to do a lot of advertising if you want it to work, and it can cost a lot of money.

Top tip:
One of the objectives of your site is to filter out
people you don't want, as much as it is to attract the
people you do want.

Despite what you may think, your website is unlikely to work best
as an advert. Read on to find out more.

Writing your Home page

"90% of web interactions start with search."
Source: Pew Internet

What are people searching for? Two things. Entertainment and information. So if that's what they're searching for...that's what you've got to provide. No-one goes to the Internet searching for an advert. They are not looking to be sold to. They are searching for information so they can make their own decision. The level of entertainment you provide varies depending on what you offer and on your brand values. (If you are an undertaker, for example, perhaps you don't want to provide entertainment.)

Unwelcome

Don't start 'Welcome to my website' – it's dated and unnecessary. Instead, make your main heading keyword-rich (the SEO section below explains why).

As you can see from the above screenshot, over 2 million people have included that phrase in their website. Over 2 million people are wrong.

In my view, your Home page copy should be about your customers more than it is about you, so they know they've landed in the right place.

So, what should you make clear on your Home page? At-a-glance, who it's for. One technique is the question-and-answer approach i.e.

- DON'T write: 'We are X, based in Y and we specialise in Z'.
- DO write something like: 'Looking for A, B or C? You've come to the right place.'

Some example Home page copy is in Appendix A.

Sub-pages

More than any other, your Home page should answer 'What's In It For Me?' from the customer's point of view, and direct them where to go next in your site. Let them know they've landed in the right place, that you understand their needs or can solve their problem.

So a key objective is to get site visitors to click through to your sub-pages. Make it clear where you want them to go. This can be done in the footer, the middle of the page or (vertically) in the right hand sidebar.

See Appendix B for examples of call-to-action graphics and text.

Newsletters

Another objective might be to capture the email address of your site visitors. They have shown enough interest to land on your Home page in the first place – whether it's thanks to your offline marketing or your SEO efforts. If they are not going to buy immediately, at least you can keep messaging them every week or month or six weeks (if you can't send something at least that often, there's no point), and then they might buy later.

In return for them signing up for your newsletter or tipsheet, you have to incentivise them with something – for example, a free ebook, white paper or downloadable report.

"91% of email users have unsubscribed from a company newsletter they previously opted-in to."
Source: blog.hubspot.com

Remember, our inboxes are full of stuff that we don't have time to read. What I would say is that – even if they don't read your tipsheet, even if they delete immediately – it still reminds them you exist, who you are, what you do and that you're still trading. You don't want them to unsubscribe so you do need to add value. Do not make it an advert or call it a newsletter; instead, make it a tipsheet that provides relevant information.

Make the signup process easy. Use a form that asks only for their first name and email address (the more data you request, the less likely people are to give it to you). Reassure them you won't sell their information, and note that the standard position for your newsletter signup is the top of the right sidebar. (There's more about web page layout below.)

Guarantee

Your Home page is also where you can include a guarantee to take away the risk – for example, '100% money back if not satisfied, no questions asked'. Make sure it's big and bold and unmissable.

Here are some examples:

Satisfaction 100% guaranteed
ABC guarantees that only fresh seasonal ingredients are used and that all our dishes are prepared according to traditional family recipes.

Risk-free money-back guarantee
When you follow our online training course, we GUARANTEE you'll pass the XYZ exam first time. If not, we'll refund 100% of your money, no questions asked. T&Cs apply.

30-day guarantee
We want you to be completely happy with your purchase, so if you return this item within 30 days of order for any reason, there's not a penny to pay. This does not affect your statutory rights.

Memberships

Adding logos from your trade or professional association/s acts as an external endorsement that you're good at what you do, because they act as a visual shortcut to decision-making. If a customer is choosing between two otherwise identical suppliers, and one shows reassuring membership logo/s and one doesn't, guess which they'll choose? Here are a few examples, to show you what I mean:

Embedding

To keep your Home page content fresh, you can embed your Twitter feed, Facebook likes, review ratings and/or blog headlines. When people visit the site they can see it's current, and Google likes it because it's constantly updated.

Twitter widget on Comms-Plus.co.uk

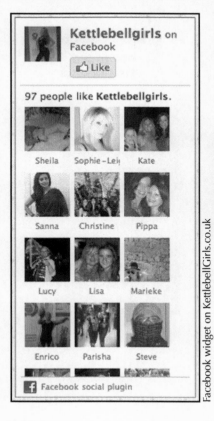

Facebook widget on KettlebellGirls.co.uk

Customer Reviews

Silicon Beach Training
★★★★★ 4.9/5 stars
Based on 22 reviews.
See independent Google Places, Free Index and Qype reviews.

Latest News

15. 11. 2012
Would You Use Microsoft Excel on Your Mobile?
Rumour has it Microsoft looks set to release a version of Office for iOS and Android devices early next year,...

14. 11. 2012
5 Management Lessons From History's Greatest Leaders
Throughout history there are certain figures who stand out as naturally great leaders. It is always useful for managers to...

Reviews & News on SiliconBeachTraining.co.uk

BLOG View all posts →

AAAH, THE DURANTE QUESTION. YOU KNOW ABOUT THAT, RIGHT?
09 November 2012

It's the unwritten rule for copywriters everywhere. We have to answer the Durante Question before we take on a job. You may not have known it existed, you may not know you're doing it – but it does. You do.

Blog teaser on ProCopywriters.co.uk

Writing your 'About us' page

Your 'About us' page is where you write about you (the clue is in the name).

Dealing with organisations via the Internet is quite a remote experience. When **you** are what you sell, you want to express as much personality as possible through the screen, so customers understand what you do, trust that you can deliver it, and like your brand enough to buy from you. (This doesn't apply to the brands that sell on their big name reputation rather than because of the people who work there.)

When I check my Google Analytics, I find my 'About us' page is the second most popular link. I bet if you check your analytics, you'll find your 'About us' page is popular too. Why is that?

I think it's because people do business with people. They don't just want to know what you sell; they want to know what kind of business they are dealing with and who's who behind the scenes.

As with all marketing communications, you have to decide what is the objective of your 'About us' page / what is your Most Wanted Response, and make that clear with a call to action.

External endorsements

If you want to engender confidence that you know what you're doing, your 'About us' page is where you do your shameless bragging. It's not the place to be modest. Include external endorsements that prove your claims, such as:

- Testimonials, reviews or recommendations

- Case studies
- Client list or logos
- Awards you've won
- Trade or professional memberships you hold

These may appear on the 'About us' page itself, perhaps as a sub-page within the 'About us' section, or even as standalone pages in the main navigation of your website.

Company history

When writing your company history, it's natural to write something like: 'We were founded in 1905 and then we bought this machine and then we grew and then we moved offices and then we launched this new product and now we do this, that and the other thing'.

Top tip: Turn it upside-down.

People are busy. They are easily bored and can click away from your site. Instead of writing in chronological order from your beginnings to today, make sure your most important information is first. Write in paragraphs of decreasing importance. Start with what you do now, then go on to explain how you got where you are today, and end with the date your business was founded, if relevant.

Meet the team

The most common 'About us' pages include pictures of key team members with a brief biography and perhaps a link to their LinkedIn profiles. It's a good idea, but note that this type of biography does not have to be a complete CV.

As when writing company-level 'About' copy, you should write in reverse chronological order. Start with what each person does now and end with their previous job history and qualifications (if relevant). You can also include a quote from them as their personal message to clients. I always recommend you include a sentence or two about their hobbies and interests outside work, to make them more approachable. I bet if you write that they always wear odd socks, once kissed Kylie and support Arsenal football team, that's what new clients will talk about before they discuss work.

People want to put a face to the name (especially when YOU are what you are selling) so include picture/s or even caricatures. Here is an example:

Top tip:
You can get caricatures drawn for you at fiverr.com for – guess what – a fiver.

Letter from the MD

Another approach for the 'About us' page is to use the 'Letter from the MD' technique. Include a picture and details of the MD's personal commitment to customers. Maybe even give their mobile phone number, for added reassurance.

Personal profiles

As with a dating site profile, your aim is to be relevant, show personality and be appealing enough for your desired customers to contact you. There's an ongoing debate about whether it's better to write profiles in the first person ("I am a copywriter") or the third person ("Jackie Barrie is a copywriter"). In my view, it's far better to write in the first person.

Some example 'About us' page copy is in Appendix C

Why choose us

When your objective is to convince new customers that you're the supplier they want, you can add a 'Why choose us' page as well as, or even instead of, an 'About us' page. List the top 10 (or 13 or 7 or 3) reasons to choose you, which acts as a shortcut to help potential customers decide.

See Appendix D for some example 'Why choose us' copy

What NOT to write on your 'About us' page

With thanks to fellow copywriter, Doug Jenner, who inspired part of this section, here are some typical examples of what NOT to write on your 'About us' page, and my explanation of why it's not helping your marketing effort if you do.

"We are passionate about what we do"
Who cares? Even when writing about yourself or your business, you have to answer 'what's in it for me' from the client's perspective. They don't care about your passion or lack of it. I regularly pass a baker's in my local High Street that claims to be 'passionate about bread'. I don't believe them. Nobody, but nobody, is passionate about bread. And, whatever they say, it doesn't tempt me in to buy a loaf. In my view, 'passion' should be saved for the bedroom (or the kitchen table...). It is an overused and irrelevant word in business.

See above screenshot that shows over 19 million results for a search of this phrase. Oh dear. Over 19 million websites could do better.

Perhaps 'passion' would be better expressed as enthusiasm – a quality that comes across more easily in video and face-to-face meetings than it does in text.

"We are highly respected"
Then prove it with testimonials and case studies. What other people say about you is more convincing than anything you can say yourself.

"We are proud that..."
Who cares how proud you are? We only care what you can do for us.

See above screenshot – over 4 million web pages brag about this. Who cares?

"We provide traditional and old-fashioned service"
Don't be general; be specific. Give examples. And only ever state things that are important to your customers.

"We provide flexible, personal, tailor-made service"
Yes, that's what service should be. Again, don't just tell us; show us what you mean.

In novels, you don't write: "He was angry"; you write: "He stormed into the room and swept all the ornaments off the shelf, shouting". You can use this 'show don't tell' technique in web copywriting too e.g. 'Your item will be protected by bubble wrap, packed into an unbranded box, carefully wrapped in brown paper, and delivered to your doorstep on the day and time that you choose. If it doesn't arrive promptly and safely, you don't have to pay.'

"Our clients have distinctly discerning and bespoke needs"
Of course they do, we all do. Do you have any clients that are exactly like me? What did you do for them? Were they happy with the results? Will you be able to do the same for me? That's all customers care about so that's what you have to tell them.

"Our clients are small, medium and large"
You will never sell to 'everybody'. It's better to target a specific niche. Anyway, it's better to give examples, list their names, or show their logos (with permission, of course).

"We work in partnership with you as an integral part of the team"
Cliché alert. These over-used statements sound too greedy to include in upfront marketing communications. They don't say anything except that you want to inveigle your way into my business so I can't get you out. I want control of deciding how closely I work with my suppliers, or not.

Over 2 million websites 'work in partnership'. Sigh.

"Only ever as good as our last job"
Cliché again. If that's really what you want to say, then tell the story of your last job. Explain what happened before you got involved, what you did and what the results were. People buy results.

"No matter how big or small"
Another cliché. Say how big or how small. Use visuals. As big as an elephant or as small as a mouse. From John O'Groats to Land's End. From the smallest sole trader to the largest conglomerate. Paint stunning word pictures for us.

"We go that extra mile / We bend over backwards"
Meaningless puffery. Don't just say it; prove it with examples.

"We would be happy to talk to you"
Of course you would. You want my money.

Breaking the rules

The web designer at ALittleBitOfSomething.co.uk has written a one-page website that oozes with personality and definitely filters out enquiries from people that won't 'get' his sense of humour. With 17,000 Facebook likes, it breaks nearly all my rules! See the screenshot on the facing page to show you what I mean:

You are not a web designer.
I am the web designer.

You wouldn't tell Mr. Marks of Spencer how to make slacks or Mrs. Audrey Audi how to build motor cars, would you? So please, Sir, don't tell me I should "bevel" things. Get back to doing what you do best and let me do the web designing.

If you take control, you'll end up with a huge lump of dog muck, and people will laugh at it behind your back. Youths will point and say:

❝ that man didn't listen to the web designer and his website looks shit.❞

All I need from you is a brief. And no, the logo doesn't need to be bigger. Pipe down and have a biscuit. Leave this to me.

Edgy web copy

Here's some feedback about this example, from my friends on Facebook:

"Just wish I could write so bluntly on my website."
"Horses for courses I suppose. I can only assume I'm not the target market. Having said that, it definitely does stand out."
"I love it. If writing is to communicate I say this guy knows and is confident in who he is and what he does and knows exactly who his target market is. Very clever."
"Oddly enough, I don't like it at all. I don't even think it's funny."
"Loved it, and will recommend it to all and sundry."

Some businesses can clearly get away with the 'Marmite' love it or hate it approach.

Writing your product pages for e-commerce

As you are closest to your own business, I'm guessing that you will find these pages easiest to write, but make sure you proofread them carefully and don't miss any marketing tricks.

Offer a choice of price points – gold, silver and bronze for example. Always put the most expensive first, so the other options seem cheaper by comparison. Later, you can up-sell or cross-sell from your entry-level offering. Think of McDonald's: "Would you like to go large?" and "Do you want fries with that?"

- DON'T say 'We sell x y z'
- DO say 'You can choose from x y z'

Pet rant: Please don't use the world 'solutions'. As you can see from the screenshot, nearly 2 billion (2 billion!) people have used that word on their website. It's tired.

Do you remember the Silentnight bed adverts that featured a hippo and a duck? Freemans used to sell cuddly toy versions of the hippo and duck, and someone wrote this description in the catalogue: 'Henry Hippo is 24 inches high and comes in his own striped pyjamas.' Oops! It fails the 'dirty mind' test.

So did their description of a JPS digital clock where they missed out the critical letter L.

TEBRO. 'Silentnight' cuddly hippo and duck — as featured on T.V. Hippo comes in his own striped pyjamas and is 24 in. high.
TX 1155   Hippo + Duck   £34·95

JPS Digital Cock. See through display. Functions include. Time display. Calendar. Alarm with snooze feature.
YG 2127 J.P.S. QUARTZ CLOCK
£14·99

The evidence (from my scrapbook)

Before starting my own business in 2001, I spent 18 years working in the home shopping sector, so there's not much I didn't learn about selling off the page (or screen).

In print catalogues, every inch of space is selling space. There's not much room for text as the pictures tell the story. Therefore the copy should only add information that's not visible in the image.

For my first writing job I had to write purely descriptive copy such as: "Black skirt with two patch pockets. Material: 50% polyester, 50% cotton. All garments washable. Please see size guides at the back of the catalogue."

Writing something short is actually harder than writing something long, so every word has to count.

I also wrote copy for Jeff Banks when he was at Warehouse. 20 pairs of black trousers had been photographed on black backgrounds, and it was impossible to see the detail. From the sample garments on the rail in the cutting room, I had to describe the differences between each pair in a handful of words.

More recently, I've written product copy for Ann Summers' catalogue. (For reasons of decency, I won't give an example here, but will happily email it to you if you're interested!)

Online, you don't have the same restrictions with word count. You might also want to include keywords to help with search. And you definitely want to allow customers to leave reviews. (These days, what other people say about your products is more convincing than anything you say yourself.)

Here's the start of nearly 500 words of web copy I wrote about a single piece of furniture, with the objective of helping people to imagine it in their own home:

The cupboard doors of this attractive larder unit open to reveal two removable shelves and adjustable shelf racks, so there's plenty of room for all those tins and packets. Below are two half-width drawers and one full-width drawer for extra storage. Your tea towels and tablecloths all tucked neatly away, perhaps. Mind you, although it's described as a larder unit, we think this painted pine cupboard could suit almost any room in your home. We can imagine it as a toy cupboard, or even a wardrobe, for example...

The full version of the copy is in Appendix E.

Hawkin's Bazaar

I love the Hawkin's catalogue, because they usually put real effort into writing interesting copy about each item. They sell retro and fun gifts, toys and games, so it's a good fit with the brand to inject a little fun into the product descriptions. Here's a great example from their current website:

Bring some beat and rhythm to your work space with this great sounding drum set you can fit on your desk. It may not look like much, but it surprised us how much you can get out of the scaled down tom-tom, pair of snares and the cymbal. You may not become a drumming sensation overnight with this mini kit, but even Phil Collins (ask dad) had to start somewhere.

- *Mini drum kit and stand.*
- *Has a tom-tom, two snares and a splash crash cymbal.*
- *Includes two drum sticks.*
- *Easily assembled in minutes without tools.*
- *Assembled drums 44cm tall.*

Hawkin.com

Land's End

Land's End famously give extra information that compels customers to buy. Here's their description of one of this season's skirts. Note the friendly tone of voice, their use of the word 'you' (which is always good), and the way they've turned features into benefits:

Put the wrap on style
The awesome look of a wrap skirt, with none of the perils. (You know what we mean.) The shape is slim and straight, with an invisible back zipper. 33% cotton/32% acrylic/20% polyester/10% wool/5% other. Dry clean. Imported.

- *Plaid fabric has tweedy texture*
- *Faux wrap style is created by a single front pleat*
- *Slimming straight silhouette*
- *Smooth full lining*
- *Modern above-knee length*
- *Approx waist to hem lengths: Regular, 22'; Petite, 20 1/2'*

LandsEnd.com

Lush

Just look at the creativity, humour and personality in this description of an avocado bath bomb from the Lush website:

Grab the avocado, olive oil and lemongrass. No, you're not going to have a salad; you're going to 'ave a bath! Use this when your skin is thirsty and your mind is blocked. If you haven't got a friend to tell you to pull your socks up and get back up and out there, then this ballistic will do the job for you!

Lush.com

What you can learn from this

Don't just take the manufacturer's spec and assume that's the best selling copy you can use. Instead, take your customer's perspective, think about what's important to them, and write your copy with that in mind.

Top tip for non-profits:
Even if you are not selling a product or service, you are still selling your organisation to supporters, fundraisers or sponsors, so the same principles apply.

Going viral

At the moment, there is a massive trend towards humour and irony in product copy. Sales are being boosted by viral reviews on Amazon and creative descriptions on eBay. These examples may be among the funniest things you'll ever read. Perhaps you can use them to inspire your own copywriting.

Bic for Girls

You might have seen the recent news that reviews for this girly pen went viral (a total of 530 on the Amazon.co.uk site at the time of writing).

Here's the official description:

A beautifully smooth ball pen designed specifically for women. The pink barrel has a great floral design that continues onto the metal cone. Super smooth Easy Glide ink & a cushioned grip make writing with this pen ultra comfortable!

Many people took offence at the idea the pen was just for women. Here's just one of the spoof reviews by Davey Clayton:

No good for man hands
I bought this pen (in error, evidently) to write my reports of each day's tree felling activities in my job as a lumberjack. It is no good. It slips from between my calloused, gnarly fingers like a gossamer thread gently descending to earth between two giant redwood trunks.

Read this and other fun reviews at Amazon.co.uk/product-reviews/B004FTGJUW

Veet for Men

Another Amazon product with reviews that went viral is Veet for Men. The original description is fine, as it spells out the benefits and usage process clearly.

Veet For Men Gel Creme is a quick and effective way to remove body hair leaving your skin feeling smoother for up to twice as long as shaving. Get smooth results in as little as four minutes, with an easy rinse-off formula that allows you to use it in the shower. No razor rash and no prickly regrowth. Leave on for between 4-6 minutes, no longer. Suitable for the back, chest, arms, legs and underarms only. Always follow the directions for use.

I daren't include the reviews (most of them are a bit rude!). If you enjoy that kind of thing, you'll find them at Amazon.co.uk/Veet-Men-Hair-Removal-Creme/dp/B000KKNQBK/ref=sr_1_1?ie=UTF8&qid=1353241140&sr=8-1 .

Three Wolf Moon T-shirt

The item that started this trend (as far as I know) is the Three Wolf Moon T-shirt. The first ironic review was by Brian Govern and ended:

<u>Pros</u>: Fits my girthy frame, has wolves on it, attracts women
<u>Cons</u>: Only 3 wolves (could probably use a few more on the 'guns'), cannot see wolves when sitting with arms crossed, wolves would have been better if they glowed in the dark.

That prompted thousands of similar reviews, and sales shot up 2,300% according to the BBC.

Read the whole story at http://en.wikipedia.org/wiki/Three_Wolf_
Moon

Ford Focus 1.8 Zetec Ghia

A user by the name of 'Pistolfeet' advertised a Ford Focus
1.8 Zetec Ghia on eBay and sold it for £1080. Here's his first
paragraph:

*If Trebor made car paint then I imagine it would look something
like the colour of this car, it's a pale minty green. I will include
some green Trebor mints in the sale so that you can compare
for yourself. Please specify if you would prefer Extra Strong
mints instead, they are white (unlike the colour of this car) but I
personally prefer them even if I do hold them partially responsible
for the decay in one of my teeth.*

The rest of the text along with comments and drawings, is at
Anorak.co.uk/278787/keyposts/the-greatest-ebay-advert-ever-the-
ford-focus-1-8-zetec-ghia-with-knickers.html, (it's well worth a
read, just for the entertainment value).

Used wetsuit

Surfer d_h_morgan advertised his used wetsuit on eBay. The
humorous copy he wrote attracted over 130,000 hits and sold
for £9,000 (apparently, he said he'd give 90% of the proceeds to
charity). His text started like this:

*"I bought this wetsuit brand-new last year and have worn it a fair
bit. When I say 'fair' I reckon about 20 times, but then probably
more like 30. A fair few times anyway. If it was not being worn, it
was hung on a hangar or rolled to prevent creasing AND I rinsed
it in fresh water after EVERY session so it's in VERY good condition*

as I look after my gear, I always do, similarly I take care of my body and shower at least once a day and always moisturise. Yes you're probably getting a feel for the kind of man I am. You can see from the pictures it has no creases and looks lovely."

If you want to read the rest (which gets a bit more risqué), it's at http://web.orange.co.uk/article/quirkies/eBay_wetsuit_listing_ goes_viral.

What you can learn from these examples is that today's customers want entertainment as well as information. They want humour as well as facts and figures. And if you are sufficiently creative with your product copy, they will pass it on to their friends. Go on, be brave and try something new. And remember that a professional copywriter can help you with that (nudge, nudge)!

Other important web pages

Landing pages (technical term!)

When people visit your site, they may not land on your Home page first. In fact, you can set up landing pages for any specific keywords or sources. For example, a page just for Twitter followers to welcome them when they've clicked a link you've tweeted. Or a page for Facebook 'likers' in Australia when they click the bespoke 'Welcome all Ozzies' app on your timeline.

I know there are not many searches for the phrase 'Bromley copywriter' and was never worried about being found on search anyway (my main route to market is word-of-mouth not SEO). Until one day when I noticed a competitor's site was appearing above mine in the search results. "Hmph, I'm not having that!" I told myself. So I put a web page together called 'What is a copywriter' that is optimised for the phrases 'Bromley copywriter' and 'Croydon copywriter'. The few people who search it will land on that page, and from there, can explore the rest of my site and book me if they want me. And, hoorah, it appears above the other guy's site.

Added value page/s

21st century marketing is about sharing not selling. So include 'added value' such as FAQs, glossary, useful articles or hints and tips. Call the page 'Resources', 'Free stuff' or 'Goodies' and see your inbound links and pageviews soar.

Blog

If you add a blog and keep it up-to-date by posting at least once a week, it will help with search (because it will be fresh content that's keyword-rich) and also human readers (because they can see the site is 'alive', get more insight into your expertise and perhaps even leave comments to interact with you). However, there's so much to say about blogging and content marketing that it will have to be a whole separate book.

What others say

Case studies or testimonials sell you better than anything you can say yourself. So if you don't include them on your website, you're missing an important trick. They can be on a separate page or scattered throughout the site. On the Analytics for one website I produced, I found that one-third of people who visited the Home page clicked the testimonials link. That just shows how much client comments mean to your site visitors.

Testimonials should not be of the 'Thanks, you were great' variety. That gives you a warm fuzzy feeling but doesn't tell prospects the story of what you did. Testimonials are better written in the format 'problem:solution:results'. State what the situation was before you got involved, explain what you did, and highlight what changed as a result. To make the page even more persuasive, you could call it: 'What our customers say'.

Top tip:
People buy results, so that's what you have to include in your testimonials.

Be customer-focused

Always put yourself in your customers' shoes. Don't bother including 'our values' and 'our mission statement'. In most cases, these should be internal documents not customer-facing ones. (And they usually only state minimum expectations anyway.) It's far better to say what you do for your customers, using language they understand and will respond to.

Contact page

It's best to use a postal address rather than a PO Box, so people can see you're real. Similarly, give your landline number as well your mobile number. Your objective here is to reassure site visitors that you're not a fly-by-night business as well as to give them ways to contact you.

You can have a contact form, but some people prefer an email address. Of course, publishing your email address online risks getting spam, so talk to your designer about ways to offset this. Whatever you do, it's hard to protect it 100%. And once your email address is out there, spammers just keep selling it on to each other. The answer is to set up a good spam filter within your email program. For PCs using Outlook, a spam filter is already built-in. For Mac Mail, I recommend Spam Sieve from http://c-command.com/spamsieve. It's $30 with a free trial – and in case you're wondering, no, I'm not on commission.

Web copy DOs and DON'Ts

Keep it simple

Because reading light on screen is harder than reading ink on paper, your web copy should be about half the length of your printed copy.

- DON'T use long paragraphs of prose
- DO use bullet points and click-through links for those who want to access more detail

READING 500 WORDS	On paper	On screen
Tired/inefficient readers	125 w.p.m. 4.5 minutes	100 w.p.m. 5 minutes
Average readers	250 w.p.m. 2 minutes	200 w.p.m. 2.5 minutes
Fastest readers	1000 w.p.m. 30 seconds	700 w.p.m. 43 seconds

Source: Malcolm Davison WritingForTheWeb.co.uk

Top tip:
500 words = 1-page A4 = 1.5 screens = 1/4 slower to read
Word count of screen text should therefore be 50% less than word count of printed text

- DO use direct language (it makes your copy more persuasive and appealing)

  - DON'T write: 'in order to allow the client to concentrate on their core business'
  - DO write: 'in order to allow you to concentrate on your core business'

- DO write as though you are talking to one person, not lots (they are reading it one at a time)

  - DON'T write 'We work closely with our loyal customers'
  - DO write 'If you want to work closely with friendly local experts, you'll find our door is always open. We're here 24/7 at the end of the phone or email ready to help you.'

- DO write so it doesn't go out-of-date

  - DON'T write 'We have been in business for 17 years'
  - DO write 'We have been providing wonderful widgets since 1992

- DO use specifics, not vague generalisations. Make sure your claims are measurable

  - DON'T write 'We're the UK's leading manufacturer'
  - DO write '9 out of 10 cats prefer us

- DON'T include irritating typos or broken '404 not found' links; it's unprofessional and annoying

Turn numbers into visuals

If you are solely describing your business in terms of numbers, it's hard for people to visualise what you mean. One technique we copywriters use, is to turn numbers into pictures.

- When I was at Freemans, I wanted to describe the weight of the daily postbag, so I phoned London Zoo and found it was equivalent to an adult male rhino. You get the idea, it's heavy!
- I wrote about the Peterborough distribution centre as 'larger than 12 Wembley football pitches – so large than some staff actually cycle from one area to another'. You get the idea, it's big!
- When talking about money, it's often measured in Mars Bars.

Pass the 'so what' test

Check that every statement you make passes the 'so what' test. Turn features into benefits. For example, a car has four wheels. So what? So it can help you get from A to B more quickly.

Pass the 'we we' test

Write from your customer's point-of-view instead of your own. To do this, you need to include the word 'you' more than you use 'I' or 'we'. For example:

- DON'T write 'We sell wonderful widgets'
- DO write 'You'll find wonderful widgets here'

You can test your web copy for the usage of 'we', 'I' and 'us' versus 'you and 'your' at FutureNowInc.com/wewe.htm.

Call to action

As with any piece of marketing, you need to tell readers what you want them to do. It might be 'Click to read more about noodle-bending', or 'Phone now to book an appointment' or 'Fill in the enquiry form today'.

Make the language strong, for example:

- DON'T write 'You can contact us on...'
- DO write 'Contact us today on...' (or, even better, 'Click the Callback button now and we'll contact you within 5 minutes / 24 hours')

These days, people resist hard-sell marketing. They just want you to provide the information they need to make a buying decision, so another effective call to action will be 'More information', 'Find out more' or 'Read more'.

Legal considerations

Mmm, cookies

You might have noticed corners or panels on many websites, inviting you to accept or opt out of cookies. (Cookies are harmless little bits of data that live on your hard drive).

PostOffice.co.uk

Most websites use cookies, even if just to capture site statistics and analytics. The warnings have been added because the EU, in their infinite wisdom, decided that everyone had to proactively decide whether to allow websites to store cookies.

They warned of fines up to £500K for non-compliance with effect from May 2012. They also said they would be unlikely to fine anyone who could prove they were working towards compliance (reading this might count).

The trouble is, in order for a website to know whether its visitors want cookies or not, it has to store a cookie. The other problem is that simple web hosting packages would need a costly upgrade to include a database to store cookie preferences.

So, at the last minute, the EU changed the guidelines. Instead of site visitors having to opt in or out of cookies, site owners can now 'presume consent'.

To be on the safe side you may wish to add a message e.g. "This site uses cookies. Find out more at AllAboutCookies.org."

Disability Discrimination Act

Your website should read OK on screen readers for partially sighted web visitors. For example, the code needs to be clean, copy should be easy to read against the background, and all images should have alt tags.

Size matters

If you give dimensions in your web copy, the EU decree that metric measurements must go first with imperial in brackets i.e. 30.48cm (12in).

Unlimited

Note that if you are a limited company it's now law that you include your registered address and number on your website (also on emails and business documents such as invoices).

Copyright

You can't copy and paste text from other websites onto your own – that's plagiarism. Similarly, you can't help yourself to other people's music and images without permission (there's more on that in the music and images sections below).

Top tip: If you want to know whether someone has scraped your own web copy, check it free at Copyscape.com.

Updating your existing website

Things change all the time, and if you're anything like me, you've probably been meaning to update your website for ages. When you get round to it, here are some of the things you need to think about.

Analyse where you are today

Look at your Google Analytics (or other webstats) to see:

- How many unique visitors your site already gets
- What keywords they search to find you
- Which page they initially land on
- How long they stay
- Which is the last page they look at
- Even more importantly, establish how many enquiries, leads, sales, and newsletter signups you get from your current site.
- This sets a benchmark that you can compare against when you launch your new site (be sure to measure using the same analytics tools before and after, so you are comparing like with like).

Check out the competition

Look at your competitor websites to see what they're up to. Chances are, they've also had a redesign since last time you looked! Decide what works for them and what doesn't, and think how your new site can stand out from theirs.

Also, look outside your industry at the websites for any brands that share your values. This is a great way to generate creative ideas for your website. (My thanks to marketing speaker, Geoff Ramm, for this suggestion.)

Set your objectives

Are you redesigning your website because you want to achieve a particular goal, or is it because you want to escape a certain problem? When you're clear about what you're trying to achieve, you're more likely to achieve a successful result. If you don't know why you're doing it; there's no point!

To paraphrase what the Cheshire Cat said to Alice: "If you don't know where you're going, any road will take you there."

To increase conversions you might want to attract more traffic (that is, more site visitors) and reduce bounce rate (that is, people who immediately leave your site because they don't find what they want straightaway).

Be clear about your brand

Offer a product or service that's in demand (if not, it's almost impossible to sell it, no matter how wonderful your website may be!)

Be consistent about the look, feel and tone of voice you use to present it, and ensure they are a good fit with your target market.

Construct your key messages in simple language, to explain why your customers should choose you.

Know your customers

Segment your market into clear customer groups, and write for each one. No-one is likely to read your whole website, and it's hard to write a single page that appeals to 'everyone'. Instead, you can construct separate landing pages for different segments of your audience. Your aim is to convince them they are in the right place, that you understand their needs and can provide what they want, and then convince them to order.

Consider the search engines

If your existing pages are getting good site traffic, you'll need to set up 301 site redirects. Make a list of the old and new URLs (web addresses) to ensure you don't miss any. Otherwise, all those visitors will get a 404 'not found' page and you'll miss out on their interest. Not only that, but it boosts your search engine ranking to have a page with lots of inbound links. If you lose the page, you could lose the ranking too.

Identify what new keywords you want to be found for, and set up separate landing pages for each one. It's hard to optimise a web page effectively for more than two or three keywords without it looking 'clumsy' to human readers.

Web design tips

Follow the F-pattern

Eye-tracking studies show that website visitors tend to glance along the top two lines of text, then scan down the left hand edge taking in only the first two words of each line, and perhaps look across the page once more. They spend very little time looking at the bottom right hand corner of the web page. The pattern of their views looks like the shape of an F.

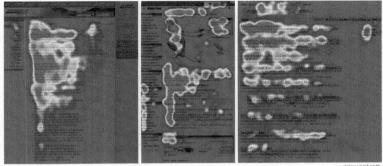

These heatmaps show eyetracking results for three web pages. In the colour version of this image, the areas where users looked the most are red; the yellow areas indicate fewer views, while the least-viewed areas are blue. Grey areas didn't attract any fixations.
Source: NNGroup.com/articles/f-shaped-pattern-reading-web-content

When you know about this F-pattern, you can arrange your content to suit it. For example, write a powerful headline at the top of the page that answers 'what's in it for me'. Add a subheading mid-way down the page, especially if the first couple of words are significant ones. And avoid putting anything important in the bottom right hand corner.

Splash pages

Have you noticed those websites that start with an animation and – if you're lucky - a 'skip intro' link? Have you ever watched the intro without skipping it? No. Me neither. This is called a 'splash page' but any extra click e.g. 'enter site' is a chance to lose site visitors. Please don't do it. The only people who benefit from splash pages are the web designers who get paid to create them.

Navigation

Aim for a site that is no more than 3 clicks deep. Here's an example simple site structure:

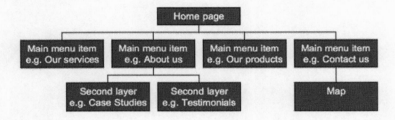

Simple site structure

Site navigation is not the same as print pagination. As pages can be read in any order, site visitors need to be able to get to anywhere, from anywhere. To do this, you can include a sitemap (this is good Google practice too) and/or breadcrumb trail, especially for complex sites with lots of pages.

Inspired by the story of Hansel and Gretel being lost in the woods, a breadcrumb trail is a set of links that show where you are within the site e.g. Home > Services > Copywriting

Breadcrumb trail on the News Shopper website (my local paper) NewsShopper. co.uk

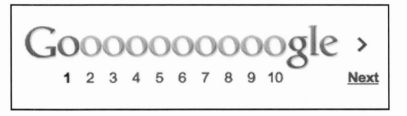

Breadcrumb trail at the foot of the Google search results page (the number of Os in Google varies depending on the number of pages it finds).

On his site WebPagesThatSuck.com, Vincent Flanders has collected some wonderful examples of what he calls 'Mystery Meat Navigation'. That is, navigation that baffles the consumer. See here: WebPagesThatSuck.com/MysteryMeatNavigation00. html.

The point is, you have to make it easy for your site visitors to find what they want. So don't let your web designer try to be too clever with the navigation they use.

Be professional

How you present yourself online and offline affects customer perception of the quality you deliver. If you want to come across as professional, a bespoke design will present your business much better than some of the free site design packages.

Similarly, you should avoid using a free hotmail, gmail or btinternet email address. Bespoke email addresses such as yourname@yourwebaddress.com are usually included free with your domain name, so there's no excuse not to have a professional-looking email address.

Choose your images carefully

Just because you can do a Google image search and find pictures doesn't mean those images are copyright-free and available for you to use. You can source images from photo libraries such as Shutterstock.com or iStockPhoto.com for a small fee (although the latter's prices have gone up since they were bought by Getty images), find something suitable on PhotoPin.com, or use your own images.

Top tip:
Teams of lawyers scour the Internet for code that's hidden within their images. They will find you and sue you if you use their images without permission. You have been warned!

Choose your colours carefully

Research colour psychology before you settle on your logo and website colours (there's lots of advice on Wikipedia at en.wikipedia.org/wiki/Color_psychology). If you're in financial services, for example, blue is a better colour to use as it means stability, whereas red means danger or debt (at least it does in the UK). The decisions you make about your brand identity should be consistent across all your marketing, not just online.

These days, a white background is considered more elegant than a coloured one. It's also easier to read. Whatever colour scheme you use, there should be high contrast between the copy and the background to comply with current web standards.

Note that only certain colours are web-safe. They are defined with a six-digit code e.g. the shade of teal I use in my logo is called #0F4A61. Catchy, huh.

Online colours are made up of RGB (red, green and blue, like your television screen). You can't use metallics or neons online, as you can with ink. You can't match Pantone or CMYK colours either. As every monitor is calibrated differently, your site colours will look different to every viewer. Just accept it, as there is nothing you can do about this.

Top tip:
Use white space to help guide the eye round the page.

Links

The default style for a hyperlink used to be blue and underlined, and purple when the link has been visited. That's no longer the case, but it's wise not to underline any text unless it is a link, to avoid confusing people. All your links should be the same format, and any text that's not a link should not be in link format. People will try clicking it, and will just get annoyed when they find it goes nowhere.

Choose your fonts carefully

These are the only fonts that work consistently across all
browsers:

Helvetica/Arial
Verdana
Courier
Times
Trebuchet
Georgia
Σψμβολ (Symbol font)

I find Verdana reads best on screen, especially at small sizes.

If you insist on using a particular house font, you can use it as
graphic text for headlines (but note it will be a graphic and not
readable by search engines). Keep your body copy in a web safe
font.

Don't use wildly inconsistent fonts and sizes, and in most cases
you should avoid **Comic Sans**, because it's perceived as amateur.

Note that anyone viewing your site can change the font size at
will, which may break your carefully constructed layout. You can't
control websites the way you can printed documents. You just
have to accept that web layouts are flexible and live with it.

Typography tips for web copy:

- Ranged left, ragged right (NOT justified). That is when the text is aligned down the left side only (it's OK aligned down both sides in narrow newspaper columns but not online where the 'rivers' of white between words make it hard to read)
- Minimal *italic*
  - Italic is fine for a sentence or two, but hard to read for more than that
- **Bold** for emphasis
  - Only use bold for headings, sub-headings, and occasional keywords
- CAPITAL LETTERS = shouting!!!
  - It has become accepted 'netiquette' (Internet etiquette) that typing in ALL CAPS is plain rude, although it can be OK for headings

Pull quotes / call-outs

You can use a technique inspired by newsprint, and highlight certain short snippets of the text by making the font larger, indented and perhaps a different colour. You can also do this to highlight short testimonials.

Pet peeve

Be sure to put the space in the phone number in the right place e.g. for greater London it should be 020 8xxx xxxx not 0208 xxx xxxx. This is a common mistake. Again, Wikipedia gives more information. Just search '0208'.

New windows

It's bad form to make site visitors open a new window or download a document without first warning them. In fact, you should only open a new window when taking them to another site. When you direct them to another page of the same site, it should open in the same window. They can use the 'back' button if they want to – apparently, it's the most used button on any browser.

Compatibility

Do make sure your site works in all browsers and platforms. More and more people are browsing the web 'on the move'. So make sure it looks OK for Internet Explorer, but also the likes of Chrome, Firefox and Safari, as well as iPads, Androids and iPhones etc.

Yvette's wedding dresses: voted the world's worst website

Standard positioning

Here's a checklist of things that have become standard in web design (although there are always exceptions to every rule):

- Logo top left, clickable link to your Home page
- Phone/email top right, so people don't have to look far to contact you
- Search box (if used) top right
- Social media icons small and bottom right, because the objective of your social media is to drive traffic to your site where you do your selling, not the other way around
- Main navigation top or left sidebar
- Newsletter/tipsheet signup top of right sidebar
- Calls to action bottom and/or right sidebar (above the fold)
- Video and/or image to catch the eye
- Main heading, one or two lines, with H1 tag
- Body copy starts above the fold, include sub-headings and bullet points for skim-reading
- Pictures to have captions beneath or to the right, also with alt tags
- Sharing buttons on every added value page, to make it easy for people to link to your content throughout their social media networks (get the code from addthis. com or sharethis.com – it's free and you don't have to register if you don't want to)
- Sitemap © Copyright information / T&Cs / Privacy policy / postal address in footer

The power of video

Our expectations of on-screen viewing are set by TV and cinema. What's more, our attention is drawn to anything that moves. You have probably noticed this when you're in a pub with a TV on in the corner, and you just can't help watching even if you don't want to. It comes from the fight-or-flight adrenaline response – if there's a snake moving in the grass, your brain is programmed to see it.

You can use this tendency to make your site come alive. Don't have wasteful Flash animations (or even worse, ghastly dancing clip-art called animated gifs) as they take up bandwidth, mobile devices can't display them and search engines can't 'read' them.

Video is excellent to include. You don't always need BBC-quality. You can record your videos cheaply on a smartphone or Flip camera, and upload them to your own YouTube channel at no cost. Be sure to add your keywords and URL in the first two lines of description (remember, YouTube is the world's second-largest search engine). You can embed videos in your website or blog simply by clicking the 'share' button.

A popular alternative to YouTube is Vimeo. Videos on there tend to be higher quality and often, more creative. Again, you can share them to your website or blog with a simple click.

Make sure your videos don't play automatically – that's just annoying, especially for anyone viewing your site in an open-plan office. And people are busy and impatient, so respect their time and keep each video under one or two minutes long. If you have longer information to impart, break it into shorter videos.

Music

Although it may be easy to add a track from iTunes onto your home-made video, you can't just help yourself to music that is copyrighted and stick it on your website. Some artists are highly litigious. They will find you and fine you for using their music without permission. You've probably noticed videos you've seen on YouTube are occasionally removed for 'copyright infringement'. You can source copyright-free music at the likes of iStockPhoto.com or get it composed for you.

Search engine optimisation (SEO) made simple

Imagine you've just searched a particular keyword or phrase, and you're looking at a page of Google results. At the top may be a tint box containing sponsored ads (those companies have paid to appear there). On the right is a column of pay-per-click (PPC) Adwords (those companies have set a budget to appear there, and it costs them money every time their ad is clicked. When the budget runs out, their ad disappears and someone else's is shown.) The main part of the page comprises the 'organic' listings, also known as the 'natural' or 'free' listings. These are the results that Google thinks match your search, ranked in priority order, displayed at absolutely no cost.

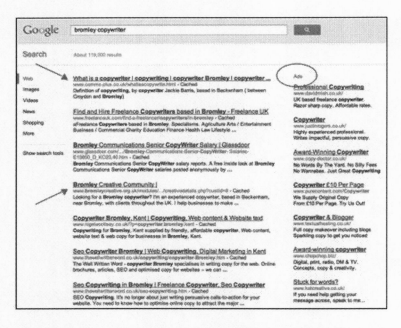

Search results for 'Bromley copywriter' showing PPC ads in the right sidebar, with my site at #1 in the free listings and my Bromley Creative Community profile at #4.

If you're anything like me, you probably click the natural links rather than the ads. And so will your customers.

The top three links in this 'free' area get by far the most clicks. What's more, any link on page 1 gets far more clicks than those on pages 2 or 3. And if your site doesn't appear in the first three pages, you might as well not be there at all.

Getting ranked

Note that no-one can guarantee your website top placement in the organic listings on page 1 (so don't believe them if they claim they can). Google's algorithm is a well-protected secret, and it changes all the time. But, broadly speaking, there are four things that Google (and other search engines) are looking for. In no particular order:

1. Good, clean code

Most websites are written in html (hypertext markup language), css, php or other code. Getting that right is down to your web designer or developer.

2. Regularly updated content

That's down to you. If you upload a site and don't change it for two or three years, it will gradually slip down the rankings. That's one reason why including a Twitter feed, blog and/or news archive can be so useful.

3. Inbound links

Each link into your site is like a 'vote' that moves your site up the rankings, especially if it's from another highly ranked and relevant site. So if you're a builder and you get a link from the florist down the road, it might not do any good at all. But if you're a wedding venue and the florist that links to you is Interflora, it might help a lot.

Note that links that go out of your site may be useful to human visitors but add no search-engine value at all. Be sure to add some meaningful copy around every outbound link you include. And don't be tempted to swap links with other websites, in case you're penalised for being a link-farm.

4. Keywords and phrases

It's more important to write compelling copy for human beings than for search engines, but here's where your web content is critical.

Top tip:
Where I refer to keywords in this book, I also mean key phrases. It's hard to be found for an individual keyword that everyone in the world is competing for e.g. 'copywriter', it can be easier to be found for a so-called 'long tail' key phrase e.g. 'copywriter Bromley'. The longer and more specific your key phrase, the better (so long as people are actually searching for it).

You can include your desired keywords in headings, sub-headings, picture captions, body copy and links. You can also include them in the meta tags.

Choosing your URL

URL stands for Uniform Resource Locator (bet you really wanted to know that, didn't you!). It's better known as your web address or domain name.

Top tip:
If you have a Wordpress blog, note that you can edit the permalinks under each post title so they are keyword friendly.

Your URL can be one of the main factors that affects where your site appears on search, so it's important to consider which domain name/s to buy. You may trade as one brand name yet use another for your website (and point one to the other, a process known as 'web forwarding' or 'site redirect').

A training company runs 11 external blogs, each with an exact match domain name, and all pointing to their main website. Each blog is regularly updated with unique content and gets found on search.

An SEO company runs an external blog called WhiteHatLinking because they know it's a commonly searched phrase ('white hat' techniques are approved by Google whereas 'black hat' techniques are not). Again, the blog content is kept fresh and comments are encouraged. As a result it appears high in Google rankings and drives traffic to their main site.

James Coakes explains: "I think there are brochure sites and marketing sites. Our brochure site is optimisethis.co.uk which clients can be sent to and it rarely changes but our marketing site is whitehatlinking.co.uk where we add content regularly.

If you have a bigger budget you can combine both strategies into one site, but for the smaller business that wants to add content themselves this is a solution that works and Google loves Wordpress."

As of October 2012, Google no longer favours domain names that are an exact match for the keyword search, unless they are backed up by quality content. So if you have bought 'locksmithsinclapham.co.uk' it doesn't necessarily mean you will automatically appear at the top of the rankings for a search of 'locksmiths in Clapham'. If your web pages also contain relevant copy about locksmiths in Clapham, then your ranking should be unaffected.

Here are a couple of sites that use exact match domains for popular search terms and contain loads of optimised content. They both appear high on a search of those keywords (at the time of writing):

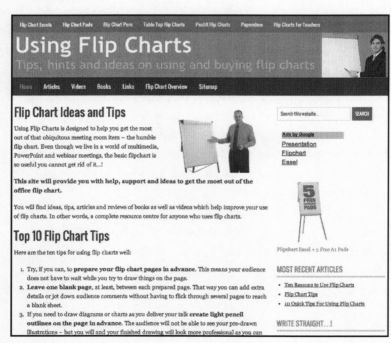

Finding your best keywords

Firstly, it's important to use customer language. For example, I heard that the DVLA used to talk about the 'road fund licence' on their website. Then they realised the rest of us call it the 'car tax disc' and had to rewrite their web copy to match.

To find out what language your customers use, search 'keyword tool' in Google and click the link:

https://adwords.google.com/select/KeywordToolExternal

It's free.

You have to wait a moment while it loads. Then you can type

in the search term/s of your choice along with the CAPTCHA code. (The CAPTCHA code is that random string of letters and numbers you have to type on some websites to prove you're a human being not a robot.) Google will return a list of suggested keywords, each showing how many times it's searched per month and how high (or low) the competition is.

A solicitor in Mitcham wanted to be found for a search of 'solicitor Mitcham'. The keyword tool showed that there was 'high competition' i.e. his competitors had already claimed that space. But he also found that lots of people were searching 'notary Mitcham' and there was low competition for that phrase. Being a notary was one of the services he provides, so he was able to optimise his site for those keywords and rake in all that business, without worrying about being found for a search of 'solicitor'.

An interior designer found there was no hope of her site ranking first for any general keywords, but that lots of people were searching for 'How to choose an interior designer' or 'interior design colours', 'interior design curtains' and 'interior design carpets'. We therefore wrote a series of blog posts with these as headings, and were able to drive traffic to her site that way.

You will probably find that 'long tail' searches are more useful. That means that it will be difficult to appear at the top of the listings for short words such as 'trainer', because everyone in the world will be competing for those. It's better to optimise your site for 'trainer Brighton' or 'social media trainer Brighton' or 'recruitment social media trainer Brighton'. The more niche, the fewer searches, but the more relevant your page will be.

One of my other favourites is GoogleFight.com. It's not affiliated with Google, but is a fun way of finding out which keyword is searched more than another. For example, try a search for 'pen' v 'sword' and see which is mightier. More seriously, I searched 'copywriter' v 'copywriting'. The winner, in case you're interested, is 'copywriting'. I also searched 'copywriter Bromley' v 'copywriter Croydon' which tells me there are marginally more searches for Croydon. These quick searches tell me how to word my own website. Why not have a little play and find out how best to word yours?

How to optimise a web page

I used to work with a particular team of web designers, and could never be bothered to look up their phone number, so I'd just search their business name on Google.

The two lines that appeared in the search results under their web link read something like: "This web-design company is run by three lesbians."

I did wonder whether that's why they designed so many construction websites, and what the clients thought of me when I turned up to meetings.

Anyway, one day, I dared to tackle the web designers about it. "Why do you consider it good marketing to have that information included in your meta-description?" I asked.

It turned out it wasn't true, and they didn't even know that's what it said. Some mischievous web developer had added it into the code without their knowledge.

I fell foul of a similar situation when I belonged to a certain business networking website, years ago. Just for fun, I'd written a profile in the form of a fake obituary, not realising that the first two lines would appear on a Google search for my name.

When people tried to find me, it read: "Jackie Barrie was today reported missing, presumed dead". If they had clicked through to the full profile, they would have soon seen that it was a comedy piece. But I'll never know how many calls I lost from people who didn't look any further.

When someone I knew rang my phone number, full of shock and concern (followed by surprise when I answered), I quickly changed the description to something more suitable.

That kind of situation is not the only reason why meta-tags are important. They are one way of determining where your site appears in the search listings. (Meta = above. Meta-tags are text that appears in the code for search engines to read but not necessarily in the web text for human beings to read.)

10 SEO tips

Without getting too techie, here are 10 things you need to do (or get your web designers to do).

1 Do your keyword research and identify which keywords and phrases you want to be found for

2 Visit your competitors' websites and click View > Source or type Control + U to see what meta-tags they are trying to be found for

3 Aim to optimise each web page for one – or at most three – keywords. Don't try to include all your keywords on one page.

4 Include your main keyword/s in the title tag (that's the text that appears in the grey bar in the top of the browser window)

5   Include your keywords in the page description (that's the bit that shows in the search results but not necessarily on the website itself)

6   Include your keywords in the main page heading, with the 'H1 tag'

7   Include your keywords as 'alt tags' for images (read by screen readers for poorly sighted site visitors). Depending what browser you use, you may be able to see the alt tags in a little pop-up window when you hover your cursor over an image.

8   Repeat your keywords within the first 250 words of copy (but without making it clumsy for human beings to read)

9   Make your keywords bold so search engines realise they are important e.g. as sub-headings (this helps humans to navigate and skim-read too)

10 Make your keywords into clickable links, which is another way to tell search engines they are important i.e. Don't use 'Click here'; instead use 'More information about keyword'

Top tip:
Do not try to fool the search engines by using white-on-white text, or by listing all your keywords at the foot of the page 'below the fold'. They are wise to these tricks. It won't help and may well get your site banished altogether.

Discovery questions

These are the questions I typically ask during an initial 360-degree 'discovery' meeting with any new client. We discuss all about them (their brand, products and services), all about their customers, and all about their competitors. I can then write in a way that includes their unique offering, makes them stand out from the rest, and encourages their target market to respond.

1. What do you sell?
This part is all about you, your products and your services. What problem do you solve or solution do you provide? Which is your core speciality? Which is most profitable (earns you most income for least effort or expense)? Do you have a range of price points (cheap, medium, high)? What market research have you done to prove there is a demand for what you sell?

> *This becomes your product/services page/s*

2. Who are your clients?
Who buys your stuff (there may be more than one group of target customers)? Which is your ideal client? Which is the most profitable type of client (either because they spend most per transaction or bring most repeat business)?

> *This becomes your Home page or Our clients page*

3. Who are your competitors?
Who else might your customers look at as well as you, if they shop around? Who else comes up on Google for a search of your keywords? Might your customers decide to 'do it themselves' rather than pay you at all?

> This is background information

4. What is your current route to market?

How do your customers find you e.g. website, cold calling, direct mail, networking/word-of-mouth?

> This is background information

5. What are your keywords?

What words or phrases do people use when searching online for your service?

> If you want to be found on search, selected landing pages can be optimised for your desired search terms

6. What is your USP?

Why do your customers buy from you instead of anyone else? What makes you different? Why should anyone give you their money?

> This may form your Why us page

7. Do you have any external endorsements?

Are you a member of any trade or professional bodies? Have you won any awards? Do you have testimonials or case studies written in the format problem:solution:results?

> This may be used on your Home page, About us page, or footer/sidebar of every page

8. What is your brand?

What are your 5 top brand values? How are they expressed in the look, feel and tone of voice of your brand (or personal) identity?

What does your logo look like? What are your corporate colours and house font? What is your strapline (if you have one)?

> *This is expressed throughout the website*

9. What is your objective?

What do you want people to do as a result of this marketing piece? What is your most wanted response? What is your desired call to action? This assumes you are producing 'direct response' advertising (where you want to get a measurable return on your investment) not brand awareness advertising (usually, only the big brands do this).

> *This is your call to action*

10. What are your FAQs?

What questions do your customers most commonly ask?

> *This may become a separate page or be answered in the general web copy*

11. What 'added value' do you provide?

These days, it's not enough to have a website full of 'sales' pages. What can you offer that other people don't, to make your website 'sticky'? If you provide added value, it encourages repeat visits, demonstrates your expertise and generates goodwill. It can also result in valuable inbound links from the social media community.

> *This may be a blog or resources section*

12. Who are you?

Who are the people behind the company (people buy from

people)? This is the 'About us' or 'Who we are' page of your website, or PDF 'Speaker profile' if you are what you are selling. It can be one of the most popular pages on your site – check your Analytics to find out. Buying 'on screen' is a remote and impersonal experience, so you want to include as much of your unique personality as possible.

> *This is the About us section of your website*

13. Who do you benchmark yourself against?
Is there another organisation (whether in your sector or not) that is already doing what you want to do? Are there some websites you really love? What about websites you hate?

> *This is background information*

14. Where is your company now, and where do you want it to be?
What are your goals and objectives over the next 12 months? 6 months? 3 months? 1 month? Are your goals SMART (Specific, Measurable, Achievable, Realistic and Time-bound) or 'heart'?

> *This is background information*

15. What do you want from me?
How can I help you?

> *This is my own call to action when I use these questions with my clients*

Continuous improvement

Check your Google Analytics regularly to see how well your website is working, and make changes accordingly. Just sign up free with your Google account, and you'll get a UA number that looks something like UA-1234567. Give the UA number to your web designer and ask them to add it to the code on every page. Or, if you're using Wordpress.org, use a Google Analytics plugin (if you're using Wordpress.com, you can't use Google Analytics but you can track Wordpress' own webstats).

Google Analytics means you can drill down to a vast level of detail about how well your website is working. It tells you which page your site visitors looked at first, how long they stayed, which page they looked at last, where in the world they are, what browser they are using, and what keywords they used to search for you. All this is valuable information for decision-making.

You may well find the vast majority of site visitors bounce away immediately because they don't see what they want. A good target bounce rate is less than 30%.

Note there is no point in having Google Analytics or any other type of webstats if you never look at them, and no point in looking at them if you don't make any changes as a result.

For example, if you do some offline marketing activity on a given date with the objective of driving traffic to your site, you'll see whether it's worked because there will be a spike in visitors the next day. Or, if you're experimenting with social media, you'll see which platforms are working for you and which are not. Or, if you've posted a blog about a certain topic, you'll see if anyone has clicked through from that post.

Top tip:
The only real measure of success for a website is how many enquiries and orders it generates, not your Google ranking.

The future of websites

Not so many years ago, businesses didn't need to worry about having a website at all. Then they realised it was essential to be found on the Internet, and reproduced their print brochures as static web pages.

The first web developers were mostly techie, and created sites that worked but maybe didn't look very pretty. Then creative web designers got involved, and built sites that looked great but maybe weren't as effective as they could be. For example, splash pages coded in Flash that can't be read by search engines or on mobiles, and that meant one extra click for human visitors before they can even enter the site, which of course is an opportunity to lose them.

Now, web marketers and SEO experts influence site design to ensure the structure is simple and easy to navigate, the code compliant, the layout clean and clear, and the copy informative, keyword-rich and with strong calls-to-action.

With the explosion of Facebook, Twitter and LinkedIn since 2009, businesses need to include 'added value' content as well as 'salesy' content, in the hope that it will be shared throughout the social media community.

So now it's important to have a blog as well as, or even instead of, a website. This keeps the content fresh and helps with SEO, as well as demonstrating your brand personality and proving your expertise to human visitors.

What's more, clients are increasingly demanding the right to do their own updates without paying professionals every time something changes, so Content Management Systems (CMS) and blog sites built on platforms such as WordPress or Joomla are increasingly popular.

But even that is changing.

As a business, you want to be found on search, and Google is still the number 1 search engine, with YouTube (owned by Google) as number 2.

Google launched Google+ in June 2011, with business pages from November 2011 and 'Search Plus Your World' in January 2012. This new personal search option means that Google will return different search results when you're logged in, based on the +1s of you and your network. That's why Google wants to know who you're connected with, so it's wise to open a Google+ account and start putting your friends into 'circles'. And it's why you need to be clicking the +1 button on all the web pages you like from now on.

With Pinterest hitting the mainstream in 2012, users started sharing images more than text. This trend is reflected in Facebook's Timeline that favours pictures and video over words. Happily for professional copywriters like me, copy is still important, but these days you really should include pictures too.

So what's coming next?

Small businesses should take a lesson from the world's biggest brands. Their websites don't even try to sell to new customers these days. Instead, they offer interaction to increase the loyalty of their existing customer base. For example, you can enter a code from the can ring-pull onto the Coca Cola website, you can play 'tweet and grow' on the Kew Gardens site, and Innocent Drinks has a whack-a-mole-style game where you smash fruit with a mallet to fill a juice carton.

Here are a few examples for smaller businesses:

- An expert in contracts has created a free glossary App, to add value and raise brand-awareness
- A security company is planning a game where site visitors have to place fire and burglar alarms on the floorplan of a warehouse, then press 'go'. If they have protected the building properly, they win. If not, fires break out, burglars break in, and they get the message that perhaps the company knows more about security than they do
- Another client sells lighting for fish and reptiles, so is thinking of adding an online aquarium or vivarium, where people have to equip the tank with the right heating and lighting, and look after their virtual pet correctly to win points and discounts

Admittedly, this approach is not right for all businesses. But what do you think – wouldn't you prefer to find a certain amount of entertainment on a website, as well as just information?

You can use ideas like this to inspire your own website. Express your unique brand personality to filter out anyone who's not your target market, add video to keep site visitors engaged, and include games and added-value content for sharing.

About Jackie Barrie

Jackie Barrie runs Comms Plus, the writing and design agency that specialises in making complex information appear simple.

Her marketing experience comes from around three decades in the industry, spanning copywriting, graphic design, print, web design, sales promotion, brand identity and much more.

She grew the business from nothing, reducing her marketing budget to zero (nil, nada, zilch) because 98% of her work now comes from repeat business and referral recommendations. It's ironic, because 'traditional' marketing is the main service she provides to her clients, yet she no longer needs to do very much of it herself.

Her 'big fish' corporate clients have included: FirstPlus, Tesco, Ann Summers, PricewaterhouseCoopers, Domestic & General Insurance PLC, Freemans and Grattan. Her 'little fish' SME (small & medium enterprise) clients range from accounts to recruitment and telecoms to training, with a sprinkling of sole traders in between.

Some copywriting highlights (so far):

- Her 'Writing Without Waffle' newsletter has won Constant Contact's 'All Star' award for four years running
- She contributes to the Huffington Post – the world's

biggest blog that reaches up to 270 million readers
- She writes a monthly 'Write Right' newsletter for Fresh Business Thinking that goes out to their 70,000+ subscribers
- She's a Diamond level author with Ezine Articles – only a fraction of their thousands of members ever attain this
- She has published two books that both reached top 10 in Amazon's sales & marketing category – *The Little Fish Guide to DIY Marketing* and *The Little Fish Guide to Networking*
- Her second book was nominated for a 2012 #bizbookaward for Small Business Trends, and ended up 11th in the marketing category

Before founding Comms Plus in 2001, Jackie worked her way up to Senior Manager level in the corporate world, with a team of 12 graphic designers and copywriters reporting to her. Some of her notable achievements include:

- Recommended stationery redesigns saving over £500K p.a.
- Managed purchasing contract worth £3m p.a.
- Organised fun day that raised over £5K for Save the Children Fund
- Co-ordinated design and print of stationery to launch a new brand
- Reduced standard letters from 864 to 537 and rewrote them to fit new house style, reducing customer complaints about unhelpful letters by one-third

Jackie has also worked as an insurance clerk, a barmaid and a tea-lady.

Her favourite aspect of employment was having an MGF as a

company car. Her favourite aspect of self-employment is not having to ask anyone for a day off.

She holds a BA Honours degree in psychology, both social – what makes people tick – and cognitive – the mental processes people go through when they read words and symbols on paper or on screen. She is also a qualified NLP Practitioner, and is particularly fascinated by the language of influence.

She hates tomatoes, alarm clocks and shoes, and likes dancing, scuba diving and making people laugh.

You'll find more of Jackie's tips at www.comms-plus.co.uk, on Ezine Articles at http://ezinearticles.com/?expert=Jackie_Barrie and you can read her blogs at http://jackiebarrie.blogspot.com and https://writingwithoutwaffle.wordpress.com.

You'll also find her on social networking sites including:

- Twitter https://twitter.com/jackiebarrie
- LinkedIn uk.linkedin.com/in/jackiebarrie
- Facebook http://www.facebook.com/jackie.barrie
- Google+ https://plus.google.com/115891804981348132
- Pinterest pinterest.com/jackiebarrie

You can phone her on 0845 899 0258 or email jackie@comms-plus.co.uk.

Appendix A: Sample home page copy

rooms2remember

rooms2remember.co.uk designed by ArtDivision.co.uk copy by Comms-Plus.co.uk

Transcript

You might have seen makeover shows on TV, where the home-owners are left with a room that's too stylised to live with. Or where the transformation is done so quickly you dread to think how long it will last. Or where the results seem so 'designy' and expensive you think you'd never be able to afford it.

Not all interior designers are like the ones you see on TV.

I have a real-life approach to interior design. During a friendly home visit, I ascertain how you live your life, how you use each room, and what your tastes and preferences are. I then present you with creative and inspirational ideas that will transform your environment without breaking your budget.

As well as helping you to create a home as individual as you are, using a professional interior designer saves you time and hassle, and prevents you from making costly mistakes.

The Padfield Partnership

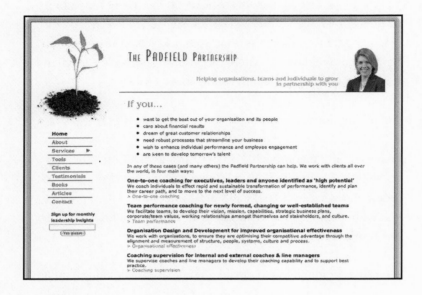

PadfieldPartnership.com by Comms-Plus.co.uk

Transcript

If you...

- want to get the best out of your organisation and its people
- care about financial results
- dream of great customer relationships
- need robust processes that streamline your business
- wish to enhance individual performance and employee engagement
- are keen to develop tomorrow's talent

In any of these cases (and many others) the Padfield Partnership can help. We work with clients all over the world, in four main ways:

One-to-one coaching for executives, leaders and anyone identified as 'high potential'

We coach individuals to effect rapid and sustainable transformation of performance, identify and plan their career path, and to move to the next level of success.

> One-to-one coaching

Team performance coaching for newly formed, changing or well-established teams

We facilitate teams, to develop their vision, mission, capabilities, strategic business plans, corporate/team values, working relationships amongst themselves and stakeholders, and culture.

> Team performance

Organisation Design and Development for improved organisational effectiveness

We work with organisations, to ensure they are optimising their competitive advantage through the alignment and measurement of structure, people, systems, culture and process.

> Organisational effectiveness

Coaching supervision for internal and external coaches & line managers

We supervise coaches and line managers to develop their coaching capability and to support best practice.

> Coaching supervision

Devant

Devant.co.uk designed by Hyde-End.net copy by Comms-Plus.co.uk

Transcript

- Do you struggle to close deals quickly because of contractual issues?
- How do you avoid getting beaten up by the other party in your contract negotiations?
- Do your sales team completely understand the words in the contracts they sign, and their impact on your business?

Delays in getting to signature can be devastating to the sales process while extensive legal wrangling can damage new commercial relationships.

Whether you're a PLC or a sole trader, the ability to execute effective contracts is key to the success of your business.

With our expertise in creating and negotiating contracts, Devant can help you do better deals, faster and more efficiently. We can also train your team in how to 'do it yourself', so you enjoy more profitable commercial relationships.

As well as providing consultancy and process development services about anything to do with contracts, we work with you to:

- Create contracts that are easy for both parties to understand and sign
- Negotiate deals that work better for your business
- Educate your staff on how to draft a contract, structure a deal and negotiate an outcome that boosts the bottom line

If you have in-house legal, we can help your team to improve contract outcomes and shorten sales cycles so you achieve more profit with less risk.

If you don't have in-house legal, you can call on our experts to draw up effective contracts for you, negotiate on your behalf, and train your team so they understand the impact of contractual terms on your business.

Call us on +44 (0)118 353 6000 for a no-obligation chat.

Appendix B: Sample calls to action

GardenGraft.com by StrayCatMarketing.com

SquireEstates.co.uk by StopTheTrain.co.uk

SecurityForum.org by Comms-Plus.co.uk

Looking for professional creative services in the Bromley area? You've come to the right place!

The London Borough of Bromley is home to a wide range of high-quality creative services, including web and graphic designers, copywriters and PR experts, photographers and videographers. When you want help from creative professionals, you can find them right here on your doorstep without paying Central London prices. Between us, we can create online and offline marketing collateral that will really help boost your business.

Find a Bromley creative – it's free! >

Are you a commercial creative professional who lives or works in Bromley? Join us at BCC!

At a time when we all have to be creative about how we win business, Bromley creatives are working together to create more opportunities for all. Simply add your details to our database for no charge, and you benefit from increased exposure to potential clients, joint venture opportunities and support from fellow Bromley creatives, as well as a powerful inbound link to your website which boosts your search engine ranking.

Join BCC today – it's free! >

BromleyCreative.org.uk on Wordpress.org copy by Comms-Plus.co.uk

Imagine-Group.co.uk by

StopTheTrain.co.uk

Assorted calls-to-action

by StopTheTrain.co.uk

Appendix C: Sample 'About us' copy

Recruit IT

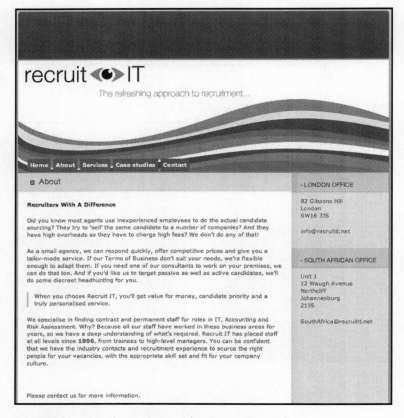

RecruitIT.net on Wordpress.com copy by Comms-Plus.co.uk

Transcript

Did you know most agents use inexperienced employees to do the actual candidate sourcing? They try to 'sell' the same candidate to a number of companies? And they have high overheads so they have to charge high fees? We don't do any of that!

As a small agency, we can respond quickly, offer competitive prices and give you a tailor-made service. If our Terms of Business don't suit your needs, we're flexible enough to adapt them. If you need one of our consultants to work on your premises, we can do that too. And if you'd like us to target passive as well as active candidates, we'll do some discreet headhunting for you.

When you choose Recruit IT, you'll get value for money, candidate priority and a truly personalised service.

We specialise in finding contract and permanent staff for roles in IT, Accounting and Risk Assessment. Why? Because all our staff have worked in these business areas for years, so we have a deep understanding of what's required. Recruit IT has placed staff at all levels since 1996, from trainees to high-level managers. You can be confident that we have the industry contacts and recruitment experience to source the right people for your vacancies, with the appropriate skill set and fit for your company culture.

Please <u>contact us</u> for more information.

Hayley Lehmann

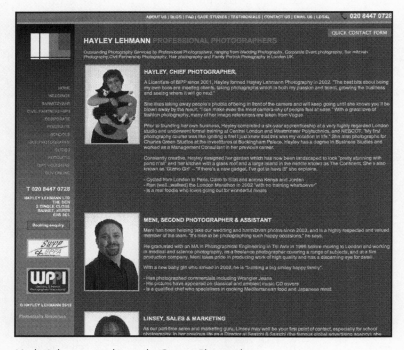

HayleyLehmann.co.uk copy by Comms-Plus.co.uk

Transcript (partial)

A Licentiate of BIPP since 2001, Hayley formed Hayley Lehmann Photography in 2002. "The best bits about being my own boss are meeting clients, taking photographs which is both my passion and talent, growing the business and seeing where it will go next."

She likes taking away people's phobia of being in front of the camera and will keep going until she knows you'll be blown away by the result. "I can make even the most camera-shy of people feel at ease." With a great love of fashion photography, many of her image references are taken from Vogue.

Prior to founding her own business, Hayley completed a six-year apprenticeship at a very highly regarded London studio and underwent formal training at Central London and Westminster Polytechnics, and NESCOT. "My first photography course was like igniting a fire! I just knew that this was my vocation in life." She also photographs for Charles Green Studios at the investitures at Buckingham Palace. Hayley has a degree in Business Studies and worked as a Management Consultant in her previous career.

Constantly creative, Hayley designed her garden which has now been landscaped to look "pretty stunning with pond n'all" and her kitchen with a glass roof and a large island in the middle known as The Continent. She's also known as 'Gizmo Girl' – "If there's a new gadget, I've got to have it!" she explains.

- Cycled from London to Paris, Cairo to Eilat and across Kenya and Jordan
- Ran (well...walked) the London Marathon in 2002 "with no training whatsoever"
- Is a real foodie who loves going out for wonderful meals

Telecoms World

TelecomsWorldPLC.co.uk copy by Comms-Plus.co.uk

Transcript (partial)

When dealing with any new organisation, you may wish to find out a bit about the people behind the scenes. Here, we profile some of our key team members, so you can get to know us. For each individual you can click through to their LinkedIn profile to check out their background, see their personal recommendations and gain confidence in their expertise. Please get in touch as we'd love to get to know you too.

Neil Barrall - Managing Director

Neil joined the Telecoms World team in 2004, and journeyed from sales director to managing director over five years. His knowledge and understanding of business telephony is second to none, and he has managed telecoms for some of the UK's largest organisations.

He says: "My passion is working with clients to enhance their business and making cost savings along the way. My clients range from public sector organisations to global businesses, each with varied requirements and telephony needs."

Neil began his career as a sales manager for Micron windows and doors. He is an avid fan of West Ham Football Club, enjoys playing golf and mountain biking.

Find Neil on LinkedIn

Appendix D: Sample 'Why choose us' copy

EcoSink

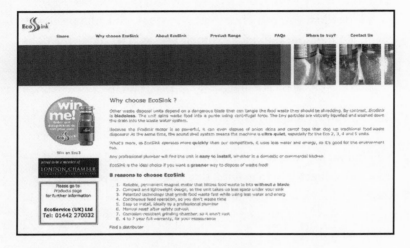

EcoServiceUK.co.uk copy by Comms-Plus.co.uk

Transcript

Why choose EcoSink?

Other waste disposal units depend on a dangerous blade that can tangle the food waste they should be shredding. By contrast, EcoSink is bladeless. The unit spins waste food into a purée using centrifugal force. The tiny particles are virtually liquefied and washed down the drain into the waste water system.

Because the EcoSink motor is so powerful, it can even dispose of onionskins and carrot tops that clog up traditional food waste disposers! At the same time, the sound shell system means the machine is ultra quiet, especially for the Eco 2, 3, 4 and 5 units.

What's more, as EcoSink operates more quickly than our competitors, it uses less water and energy, so it's good for the environment too.

Any professional plumber will find the unit is easy to install, whether in a domestic or commercial kitchen.

EcoSink is the ideal choice if you want a greener way to dispose of waste food!

8 reasons to choose EcoSink

1   Reliable, permanent magnet motor that blitzes food waste to bits without a blade
2   Compact and lightweight design, so the unit takes up less space under your sink
3   Patented technology that grinds food waste fast while using less water and energy
4   Continuous feed operation, so you don't waste time
5   Easy to install, ideally by a professional plumber
6   Manual reset after safety cut-out
7   Corrosion-resistant grinding chamber, so it won't rust
8   4 to 7 year full warranty, for your reassurance

Find a distributor

Appendix E: Sample (long) product copy

Living Creations

Standalone larder unit built in solid pine with wooden knobs

The cupboard doors of this attractive larder unit open to reveal two removable shelves and adjustable shelf racks, so there's plenty of room for all those tins and packets. Below are two half-width drawers and one full-width drawer for extra storage. Your tea towels and tablecloths all tucked neatly away, perhaps.

Mind you, although it's described as a larder unit, we think this Mottisfont painted pine cupboard could suit almost any room in your home! We can imagine it as a toy cupboard, or even a wardrobe, for example!

However you plan to use it, we believe in offering the ultimate in customisation, so you can enjoy a unique piece of furniture that's entirely to your taste.

For example, with this larder unit you can opt for a mellow wax finish for the glow of natural wood, or it can be painted in cream, white, blue or green in accordance with your décor. If you choose the resilient painted finish, you'll notice it's slightly distressed and then waxed to give a silky look and feel.

Not only that, but you can choose between wooden knobs or metal handles, whichever you prefer. And if we don't offer exactly what you want as standard, simply email us about our bespoke service, and we'll do our best to provide what you need.

We find that our customers adore the Mottisfont painted pine range because of its stunning design, beautiful detailing and solid pine and oak construction (you can be confident you're buying a quality piece of furniture, with no sneaky veneers). We're sure you'll love it too.

You can't help but admire the country styling and beautiful detailing! Every piece is crafted by expert woodworkers, with mortice and tenon joints on all doors, and dovetail joints on all drawers. We're confident you'll appreciate the high standard of workmanship! And the exceptional quality will last a lifetime (or more), making this larder unit excellent value-for-money.

Order now! The Mottisfont painted pine range is proving phenomenally popular.

Please note that this Mottisfont painted pine larder unit is usually delivered unassembled. If you would like us to assemble it for you, that's fine! Just let us know when you order.

Mottisfont painted pine furniture enhances your kitchen, living room or bedroom

With so many items in the Mottisfont painted pine range, it's possible to furnish almost your entire home with matching pieces!

If you like this Mottisfont painted pine larder unit, why not check out the matching range that includes: CD racks, coat racks, magazine racks, wine racks, shoe racks, mirrors, hanging shelves, dressing table stools, display cabinets, bedside cabinets, bathroom cabinets, corner cupboards, side tables, bookcases, writing tables, coffee tables, TV units, blanket box, hall tables, cupboards, filing cabinets, pedestal desks, chest of drawers, beds, tables, dressers, dresser bases, wardrobes and island units

Lisa Lumm LivingCreations.co.uk copy by Comms-Plus.co.uk

YOUR NOTES

6295824R00063

Printed in Great Britain
by Amazon.co.uk, Ltd.,
Marston Gate.